1 SAMUEL

A BIBLE STUDY GUIDE FOR YOUTH CELLS

1 SAMUEL

A BIBLE STUDY GUIDE FOR YOUTH CELLS

First edition 2010

ISBN 978-1-4461-5701-5

Written by Paul Franklin
St Andrews Vicarage
38a Saddleton Road
Whitstable
Kent
CT5 4JH

paul-franklin@live.co.uk

Published by Lulu (www.lulu.com)

HOW TO USE THIS GUIDE

This leader's guide has been designed as an aid to youth leaders or young people who lead groups of teenagers in any kind of Bible study. It's ideal for those who run youth cell groups or teenage house groups.

Those of you who are running youth cell groups will find this book invaluable for helping you to plan and run the word and worship sections of the cell group, whether you do this yourselves or hand the material out for others to deliver. However you may want to continue to have a separate icebreaker and to ensure that the cell are engaging suitably with witness or works activities as well.

Whichever way you choose to use and engage with the material please note that you still need to prepare carefully. Whoever is leading a Bible study should always have read the passages in advance and thought through what God might be wanting to say to *this* group at *this* time. Always feel free to adapt and change the material and to follow the Holy Spirit's leading. Teaching a group is a privilege and a joy and there are few short cuts.

That being said a good Bible study can be hard to lead so this material should take most of the pain out of the process. For teenagers there need to be a range of different activities and approaches: fun, discussion, creativity and interaction are key. That's what these sessions are all about. They contain the spice that really will help any Bible study to go well so that the group members both learn more effectively and have more fun. Do check that you have all the materials you need in advance of each session and do this with plenty of time to spare. Some sessions need a little more preparation than others. Few can simply be read through half an hour before the session is due to happen.

I should also mention that the sessions do not tell you exactly what to teach. They don't contain any really deep theology and some difficult questions are asked but not answered. Sorry if this is frustrating but it can be too easy to provide answers for ourselves or young people. Instead we need to wrestle with some of these issues and work things out as individuals or as communities. You as the leader will need to work out what you think the Bible is teaching as you work through the passages. Often the sessions do contain some suggested areas to focus on and some clues to start you on this journey.

This guide works through the book of first Samuel, covering the stories of Samuel and Saul and the start of David's life. These characters are colourful and fascinating, rich and complex. Each story has an element of awe and unexpectedness about it. Our job is not to explain it away but to allow the word of God to teach us and ask questions of us about our character and attitude, our image and identity, our successes and failures.

I hope that you and your group have loads of fun and encounter God powerfully as you interact with the book of 1 Samuel!

Faithfully,

Paul

THE SESSIONS

SESSION 1: THE DRUNK WOMAN

SET THE SCENE

Quickly remind the group where this story is set in the Bible timeline. Draw on a whiteboard or on sheets of paper:

- An apple – Adam and Eve
- A boat or rainbow – Noah
- Some stars – Abraham
- A coat – Joseph
- Pyramids – Moses
- A sword – Joshua
- A horn – Gideon
- A strong arm – Samson

Explain that the story of Samuel happens after all of these. Samson and Gideon were some of the judges who were individual heroes who saved Israel from surrounding nations. Samuel is the last of the judges, but gets his own books!

ACTIVITY: I'M BETTER THAN YOU!

Carry out a trivial game of skill such as kick ups, races, a target game, etc. Encourage the winners to mock the losers as much as they can. Ensure that the losers know this is all in good fun and part of the game.

READ

1 Samuel 1:1-8

OPENING QUESTIONS

Notice how Hannah is unable to have children but Elkanah's other wife, Peninnah has many.

- Why would Peninnah provoke Hannah about this?
- Do we ever provoke others about our success or abilities?

- How have we done this or seen others do it and why do we do it?
- Have we ever prayed really passionately for something because someone has something that we don't? Is this ok?

DRAMA: DRUNK IN CHURCH

Split the group into smaller groups and ask them to act out the following scenario:

> Someone comes into church on a Sunday morning and is acting quite strangely. It seems likely that they are drunk. Act out what might happen and how the other people at church might respond.

READ

1 Samuel 1:9-20

WORSHIP: ANSWERED PRAYER

Hannah is so passionate in her prayer that Eli thinks she's drunk! However Hannah's prayer is answered. God gives her what she asks for. Often we pray for things and sometimes those prayers are answered. Encourage everyone to think about one prayer that has been answered for them. Then go round in a circle and encourage everyone to say a short thank you prayer out loud for it. This could be done as part of a time of sung worship.

SHARE: BROKEN PROMISES

Share a time when you have broken a promise and give people a few moments to think about when they or someone they know broke a promise. Give everyone opportunity to share and ask how it feels when we break our promises or when other people break their promises to us.

GAME: HE'S NOT READY!

This game is very simple. One person in the group has to answer every question they are asked with the same statement each time: 'he's not ready'. The group have to try to get the person to smile by asking more and more amusing questions. For instance someone could ask "why haven't you kissed David?" and the respondent would have to say "he's not ready" without even smiling. As soon as they smile someone else gets to answer the questions and so on around the group. You could play using different responses. However the point of the game leads into the next Bible passage which seems to indicate that Hannah might herself respond with "he's not ready" when it comes to delivering Samuel to the temple.

READ

1 Samuel 1:21-28

DISCUSSION: PROMISES TO GOD

Hannah must have been tempted to break her promise to God and to keep Samuel. In verses 21-23 it does seem that she is being reluctant to hand Samuel over, but eventually she does follow through with her promise. We often make promises to God in the course of our Christian life. Read these out one by one and ask the group if they have ever made this promise:

- I will pray and read my Bible every day
- I won't ever do that particular thing again
- I'm entirely yours and I will go wherever you want me to
- I will be more committed to church

Were they able to keep these promises? What happened? Are there other promises we often make? What about those we sing: 'I'm gonna be a history maker in this land' for instance? Are we serious about these? Do you think God minds when we break our promises to him?

CHALLENGE

The whole focus of the first chapter of Samuel helps to remind us of God's faithfulness. God answers Hannah's prayer and Hannah has to decide whether she will keep her promise to God. God never breaks his word – he always keeps his promises. We are slightly less reliable! Encourage the cell to make one promise to God that they will definitely keep: to read their Bible once this week, to pray for a couple of minutes tonight, etc. Whatever it is keep it small and achievable!

SESSION 2: THE WHIPPING BOY

SET THE SCENE

Remind the group about what we looked at last week. Samuel is set after the time of Moses, Joshua and the Judges (such as Gideon and Samson). In fact, Samuel is the last of the judges (heroes of Israel). We saw how Samuel's mother prayed desperately for a child and how God answered her prayer. We also saw that Hannah kept her side of the bargain and gave the child completely to God, to serve in the temple.

DRAMA: BULLIED AT HOME

Split the group into small groups of three or four. Give them the following scenario and then give them some space to rehearse a short drama and perform it back to the rest of the group:

> One of you is an adopted child and the other two bully them. They do everything they can to ensure that the adopted child is miserable and treated badly. The parents won't do anything about it.

READ

1 Samuel 2:12-26

OPENING QUESTIONS

Notice how it isn't mentioned that Samuel was bullied by the other two children of Eli, but clearly they were bullies by the way they behaved to others.

- Do you think Samuel would have suffered at their hands?
- Why do you think Eli's sons behave so badly to everyone?
- Do you think Samuel is ever tempted to try to fit in or impress them?

- Have you ever known any bullies – why do they do what they do and what's the right response to them as Christians?

GAME: MAFIA!

Give each group a piece of paper with a word written on it. Most of the group should have the word 'villager'. A couple should have the word 'mafia'. Tell them they need to keep quiet about what's on their paper. Then the whole group close their eyes and you narrate the story: 'It's a cold evening in the village and all the villagers are sleeping. Unknown to them the mafia are on the loose. Could the mafia please open their eyes?'. At this point the people who are the mafia should open their eyes. You then say 'Could the mafia please choose someone to kill?'. The mafia point at a suitable target. You then ask them to close their eyes and tell the group that 'Morning has arrived. It's a new day and someone has died!' Explain who was killed and then let the group decide if they can who the mafia might be. They get to vote on one person. Whoever they choose is out of the game whether they are mafia or not. Then another round is played until either the mafia or the villagers win. Explain that this game is all about getting away with something. Some people treat life like that: as if we can get away with stuff. But God sees everything we do.

READ

1 Samuel 2:27-36

DISCUSSION

It seems that while Eli's sons seem to think they are getting away with their behaviour they are not escaping God's judgement.

- Why is God so angry with them?
- Do we ever commit sins that disrespect the worship of God? What?
- Is God's judgement fair or does it seem a little over-harsh?

GAME: HEARING CLEARLY

One person from the group is blindfolded or they could just stand facing a wall so they can't see anyone else. The leader then points at one of the other people in the room. They have to say something but to disguise their voice while doing so. See if the blindfolded person can guess who spoke.

READ

1 Samuel 3

SHARE: WANTING TO HEAR GOD'S VOICE

This is a passage that is really well known. God speaks clearly to Samuel and Samuel listens. Notice how Samuel is basically the whipping boy of the temple, running to Eli every time he calls. Notice also how Samuel describes himself to God as 'your servant'. Are we servant-hearted? Do you think seeing ourselves as servants of God might be a necessary part of hearing God speak? Ask the group what they would really like to hear God's direction on at the moment. Maybe they could share those things with each other.

WORSHIP: LISTENING

Encourage people to find a quiet space to think through how servant hearted they are and to listen to God for five minutes, possibly with music playing softly in the background.

CHALLENGE

The passage today looks at how Samuel really grows up learning to serve in the temple. It seems that this does something healthy for his character: his early life as a whipping boy puts him in a good place to see himself as God's servant rather than getting too proud. So in what ways are we serving others in the church? What menial or thankless tasks do we do just in order to serve God? What kind of things could we take up? Encourage all the cell members to think through what their act of service is, and to commit to one if they don't currently have one.

SESSION 3: GOOD LUCK?

SET THE SCENE

Remind the group how we learned about Samuel having grown up as a servant in the temple, whether he had any choice or not! Whatever we feel about that it ensured Samuel's character was quality enough for God to use him powerfully. Meanwhile Eli's sons were evil and abused their position as priests. God prophesies his judgment on them.

ACTIVITY: MAKE AN ARK

Ask the group what they know about the ark of the covenant (sometimes called the ark of the agreement). Explain that this was an object which was made at the time of Moses and which symbolised God's presence. People weren't ever meant to touch the ark – it was the ultimate holy object. Now tell the group to listen to what the ark looked like and then split them into two groups. Give each group some playdough or card/craft materials to see if they can model the ark accurately simply from hearing the description contained in Exodus 25:10-22. Don't let them see the picture of the ark here – they only get to hear the description! Closest to the actual way it should look (see picture) wins!

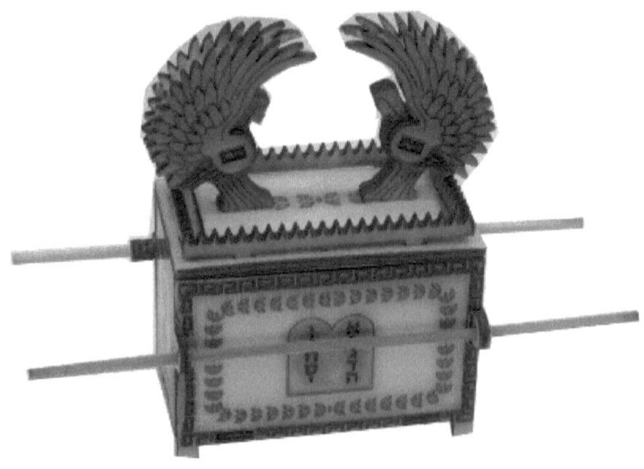

READ

1 Samuel 4:1-11

OPENING QUESTIONS

Notice how the Israelites seem to think that they need God's help to win the battle and so they fetch the Ark.

- Was this the wrong thing to do? Why or why not?
- Why doesn't God let them win the battle?
- Won't it reflect badly on God to let the Ark be captured?

ACTIVITY: CARD GAMES

Play a couple of quick card games which are heavily reliant on luck. See who is the most lucky person in the group. Ask them who believes they are lucky and who thinks they tend to be unlucky? Are Christians allowed to believe in luck?

DISCUSSION

Type or write out the following items and ask the group how Christians might sometimes be tempted to use them more as good luck charms than as symbols of God's presence:

- A Bible
- A Christian fish on a car
- A WWJD bracelet
- A quick prayer
- A cross on a necklace / Christian jewellery
- Any others?

Ask what we can do to ensure that we are not trying to use items like these as 'magic items'? Have we ever had a Christian good luck charm? Explain that there is sometimes a temptation to use holy things (even things like prayer and worship) to twist God's arm into something. However, they are not magical things – they are about our relationship with God. Without our relationship being good the things in themselves are useless.

GAME: HANGMAN

Play a quick game of hangman using the word 'ichabod'.

READ

1 Samuel 4:12-22

SHARE

Ask the group when they have lost or misplaced something that was really important to them. What did it feel like? Note how Eli seems to fall off his seat when the ark is mentioned, not his sons!

DISCUSSION

How would we know if 'the glory of the Lord has departed'? What a worrying statement! Ask the group to either go high or low to indicate their agreement or disagreement with each of the following:

- I've felt something of God's glory before
- I can tell when God is doing something powerful in a place and when he's not
- If God's glory is in a room everyone in the room feels it
- God is everywhere so its silly to talk of his glory as if its there or not there. Its always there whether you think you feel it or not!
- Its been ages since I felt the glory of God

Explain that there is a difference between the general presence of God which is everywhere and in all creation and the special or manifest presence of God which is only present in certain times or places. The glory of God is very real and is often felt by many people – even if not all. When Christians worship we should hope and pray that God's presence is real to us.

WORSHIP: GOD'S GLORY

Enter a time of worship (ideally sung) where there is a theme around the glory of God being present. Before you sing get every person to pray for each other to feel something of God's glory as you worship. Pray passionately for an encounter with the glory of God this week and in coming weeks as you meet as a group.

CHALLENGE

If we thought that the glory of God had departed from our church how might we go about getting it back? What kind of action could we take? Would it be worth the cost?

SESSION 4: NO RIVALS

SET THE SCENE

Remind the group how last week we looked at the Israelites losing a battle to the Philistines, and how the ark was stolen by the Philistines. This was a tragedy for the Israelites – the ark symbolised God's presence. Now the glory of God had departed. There seemed to be nothing they could do. There seemed to be nothing that Samuel, their leader at the time, could do.

READ

1 Samuel 5

DISCUSSION

It seems that God doesn't like to be put alongside other gods, even those of other nations who may not know any better. This may not be politically correct nowadays but:

- What should be the Christian response to those who are from other religions?
- Can we speak of 'our God' and the 'Muslim God' as if they both exist or are the same thing?
- Isn't it arrogant to suggest that our God is real and everyone else isn't?

Note that God himself deals a particular way with those of other religions but no-one has to fight his corner for him! If we think we are defending God or that he in some way needs our help then we have gone badly wrong. This passage shows us again and again that while the incompetent Israelites couldn't hold on to the ark, God is more than capable of getting it back to Israel himself!

GAME: TIME BOMB

Throw a ball or bean bag from person to person while the leader counts down silently. When ten seconds are up the leader shouts 'boom' and whoever is holding the object or catching the object at that moment is out of the game. Keep playing until only one person is left. Explain that just like the time-bomb the

Philistines really want to get rid of the ark. It's bad news and its deadly. According to an ancient text in one place it inflicts the men of the town with tumours of the groin! No wonder they want rid of it!

READ

1 Samuel 6:1 – 7:1

DISCUSSION

Ask people to move to one side of the room or the other when they hear the following statements depending on whether they agree or disagree with them:

- God sometimes causes suffering in the world.
- God hates muslims.
- Natural disasters might be caused by God as part of his judgment on nations.
- Suffering helps people to turn back to God.
- The devil causes most of the suffering in the world.
- Everything that happens in the world is part of God's will.
- God sometimes inflicts disease on people as a judgment for sin.
- When we pray for people to be healed we should also encourage them to repent.

These are not easy questions so ensure you allow plenty of time for the group to discuss them. Bear in mind that many Christians disagree with the answers of these, at least in the emphasis they place on them. However the passage today suggests that some disease is a judgment from God. Check out 1 Sam 6:9. The wise advice of the Philistines is to check whether this is co-incidence or not. It seems that it is not! However, some disease is against God's will. Many of the disasters and situations in the world make God cry and are a result of human sin or of fallen creation. We need to care deeply for the people involved and leave any judgment to God himself.

WORSHIP / PRAYER: THE WORLD

Play some music quietly in the background and place some of today's newspapers amongst the group. Encourage them to browse the stories in the papers and to say short prayers for the people and situations they read about. Do this in a relaxed and informal way, just allowing some space for the group to pray for the world.

GAME: NO RIVALS

Encourage a form of play-fight where the two contestants have to try to knock the other one to the ground. A possible way to do this is for people to rest on all fours on their backs but to keep all other parts of their body off the ground. The first one who touches the ground with another part of their body loses. Or alternatively have people hold their ankles tightly with their hands and try to knock the other person over. If they let go of their ankles or get knocked over then they lose. Play this until you have a clear winner.

CHALLENGE

The whole lesson today is that God will clearly accept no rivals. When it comes down to it between religions or beliefs only one can be left standing as the truth. But that's not just true in terms of religion, its also true in our own lives. Sometimes we might try to put him alongside other parts of our lives and leave him there. Ask the group to share the following:

- If someone saw your bedroom would they know you were a Christian? What would your CD or DVD collection say? What objects dominate your room? Where is your bible kept?
- If someone was to follow you around for a week how much of a priority would they think God had in your life?
- What can you do to ensure that God does come first? What should every Christian do to make sure they are keeping God a priority? Where does church come into this?

SESSION 5:
SOME GOOD ADVICE

SET THE SCENE

Remind the group how the Israelites lost the ark to the Philistines, and how the Philistines want to get rid of the ark because it brings disaster on them so they send it back to Israel. All during this time Samuel is still in charge of Israel. Now the ark is back – the symbol of God's presence is back! – what does Samuel do?

READ

1 Samuel 7:2-6

OPENING QUESTIONS

Note that even while the Israelites think they are seeking and trusting God they are still holding on to small gods (baals) and other symbols of luck or magic. It's possible for us as Christians to do the same. Many people will say that they are trusting God with something but secretly they are also relying on some other things too. Place the following statements around the room and encourage the group to stand by the one which they are most tempted to place their trust in if God seems distant?

- Our own abilities
- Friends
- Money
- The 'real' world
- Family

Ask if there is anything else people are likely to place their trust and hope in when God seems distant or not to care. In reality do we think these things are more faithful than God? If so it's possible we have sinned and need to think again (repent)! In this passage the Israelites did just that: putting their other stuff away and trusting only God. So they start by following Samuel's advice.

QUIZ: SCARY NOISES

Record some scary or unusual noises and play them back to the group. See if the group can identify what they are. You may be able to get suitable sound clips off the internet for this or record your own. You may like to share a story about the worst thunderstorm you've been in or about a time you heard a noise that scared you. In the next passage we see how God uses a loud noise to scare the Philistines into submission in response to the prayers of the Israelites.

READ

1 Samuel 7:7-17

ACTIVITY: AGONY AUNT DILEMMA

Following such an impressive victory you would think that Samuel would have won the respect of the people and that they would listen to him. However it doesn't turn out quite that simple! Hand each member of the group two pieces of paper and a pen. Ask them to write on one of the pieces of paper a short problem that might be submitted to a magazine's agony aunt. For instance: 'Dear Aunt Mabel, I'm having real trouble with my boyfriend. Every time he sees me he wets himself. It started off being funny but now its just embarrassing. What should I do?'. Their questions could be about anything but the more amusing the better. On the second piece of paper they should write a likely response from the agony aunt such as 'Well dear the best solution is probably if you wet yourself when you next see him so he knows how you feel.' Again, the more amusing the response the better. Now mix up the problems and responses so that they aren't paired correctly. Each member of the group could read out the problem and unrelated response. Hopefully at least some of these should be very amusing!

ACTIVITY / DISCUSSION

We may not be daft enough to take agony aunt columns too seriously but do we tend to agree who we'd seek advice from on different things? Is it annoying or good when we get offered advice, even if we don't want to hear it? Get the group to think about when they do or don't accept advice. Hand out the advice table (on a following page) and use it to start a discussion about whose advice we actually listen to. Explain that in the following passage the Israelites have to work out whether or not to listen to Samuel's advice and they choose not to despite the consequences.

READ

1 Samuel 8

DISCUSSION

- Why do the Israelites want a King? Are these good reasons?
- Why is God angry with the Israelites?
- Does God's response in v.22 surprise you? Why does God allow this?

GAME: WHO'S IN CHARGE?

Send one person out of the room and the rest of you stand in a circle. One of you is chosen as the leader. When the person returns to the room they stand in the middle of the circle and the leader mimes various actions (playing instruments, hopping, putting arms in the air, etc) and all the other people in the group have to quickly copy them. The person in the middle has to try to work out who the leader is. Play this a number of times and see if you can fool the person in the middle as much as possible. Explain that in our lives and in our churches there is a question about who is really in charge. Are we ourselves in charge? Do we want other leaders to be in charge (however good they are) or do we actually really want to leave God to be in charge? How would that feel?

WORSHIP: GIFT LIST

Whether we can get our heads around it or not, God does listen to what we want and sometimes he lets us have it, even if its not the best thing for us! That's like a loving parent. He won't just ignore us – he listens. He might tend to gently dissuade us. He might say no. But he does listen and take our wants and needs into account. Is there anything we desperately want in life at the moment, anything we'd like to really ask God for? Give each person an opportunity to write or draw whatever it is on a piece of paper and to place it in an offering bowl. Sing some songs about us seeking God's will, or about God's love for us. 'Father of lights' might be an ideal song for this time.

CHALLENGE

This week seek out someone you trust and chat to them about an area of your life that might need a little improvement: schoolwork, attitudes to parents or brothers/sisters, dealing with laziness, etc. Ask their advice on the issue and if it seems to make sense why not try to put it in action!?!

Advice

Possible sources of help: Friends, Parents, Brothers/Sisters, Grandparents, Youth Leader, Teacher, Internet, Media, Other.

Situation	I would ask...
You've spilt something on your favourite top and you need to get it out before it stains.	
You really like someone and think they might like you, but you're not sure how best to ask them out.	
Your friend is really depressed and is saying they don't want to go on living. You don't know how to help them.	
You're being bullied at school.	
You don't know what options / courses to do at school / college.	
You want to know how to cook something really nice as a meal for someone special but you're not sure how to go about it.	

You need advice on issues relating to ‘growing up’...	
Your computer is doing really strange things and you’re not sure how to fix it.	

SESSION 6: LOST DONKEYS

SET THE SCENE

We have seen how Samuel has led the nation of Israel wisely for a number of years but the people finally asked for a king so they could be like other nations. Today we meet the first of those kings, and learn a little bit about him.

READ

1 Samuel 9

GAME: FIND THE DONKEYS

Hide a number of pictures of donkeys around the meeting room or another space you have access to. Either play as individuals or as two teams – the team who find the most donkeys win the game!

OPENING QUESTIONS

It takes Saul a number of days to search for the donkeys, and initially it seems like the whole search was pointless.

- Have we ever been on a long journey or looked for something for a number of days?
- How do you think Saul feels as he carries on his search for the donkeys?
- Samuel makes a big effort to make Saul feel special. How do you think this would make Saul feel?
- Have you ever been surprised at how welcome someone has made you or how friendly they've been? When was the last time that happened to you?
- When was the last time you surprised someone else be being over-generous or treating them in a special way?

GAME: HEADS OR TAILS

Play a few games of heads or tails. The game works by everyone standing up and placing their hands on either their head or their backside, depending on whether they think a coin toss will result in heads or tails. The leader then tosses a coin and tells everyone the outcome. Those who got it wrong are out and sit down. The others carry on playing until only one winner is left. Obviously this game depends purely on probability and chance. It would be strange if someone in the room really knew what the outcome would be every time!

READ

1 Samuel 10:1-8

DISCUSSION

Note how specific the prophecies are in this passage. This is not vague 'I see a blue sky and you smiling...' sort of stuff. Real prophecy can be uncomfortably specific. It probably freaked Saul out – he wouldn't have come across a prophet before. Even more amazing is that Samuel is prophesying that Saul will be king over his people! He only came to find his donkeys! Have we ever received a prophesy from anyone? Was it specific or helpful or was it vague or unhelpful? Give time for the group to share their thoughts and experiences of prophecy. You may want to explain a little bit about how the Holy Spirit gives prophecy as a gift to us as Christians sometimes, and that is very different from fortune telling or chance predictions! Prophecy is more about communicating a message from God than it is about foretelling the future. Here though Saul needed specific confirmation about the calling God was placing on his life so he gets a bit of both!

READ

1 Samuel 10:9-13

DISCUSSION

Note that everything happens as Samuel has prophesied. Note also that God changes Saul's heart in some way! Saul joins in dancing with the prophets, much to the amazement of the people who knew him well! It seems this was more than a little out of character for him. This is a good opportunity to discuss whether the group find some things hard to do in worship (such as praying out loud or raising their hands during sung worship). Why is that we find these things hard or out of character for us? What has been the most embarrassing worship situation we've ever been in?

GAME: HIDE AND SEEK

Play a quick game of hide and seek where one of the group hides somewhere in the house or garden and the rest of the group have to find them.

READ

1 Samuel 10:14-27

DISCUSSION

Notice how Saul initially gets loads of confidence and dances with the prophets, much to the amazement of his friends. However, he seems to go really shy at the moment his kingship is to be announced!

- Why do you think Saul hides?
- Have we ever felt so afraid that we just wanted to hide from everyone?
- How do you think Saul feels when he is found?
- Are there areas in our lives where we need more confidence to do what God is calling us to do?
- Note how some people really don't like the idea of Saul being king and they criticise him. Do other people erode our confidence? How should we respond?

WORSHIP / PRAYER: CONFIDENCE

Ask each person to share some area of their life where they need more confidence and then as a group just pray for them. You can keep this simple. Maybe stand in a circle and the person on the left prays for the person on their right. Then you could finish with some appropriate songs.

SESSION 7: THE NEW LEADER

SET THE SCENE

Remind the group about how this normal guy Saul was selected to be the first king of Israel. Saul was filled with the Spirit, and had a change of heart. He also lacked some confidence from the start, being a little insecure. Today we see what happens as he takes the reigns as the new leader of God's people.

ACTIVITY: RATE THE THREAT

Collect together ten different items such as power tools and kitchen implements and ask the group to rate them according to which they think would be the most threatening and which are the least threatening! Ask the group to share what the worst punishment they've ever received is – at school or home? What is an effective threat for parents or teachers to use? You could ask them to put the following punishments in order of how severe they think they are, or which they think are the worst threat:

- Having to do all the washing up for a week
- Being grounded for a week
- Having to wash the car
- No TV or internet time for a week
- Losing your pocket money for a month
- Having your mobile phone confiscated for a fortnight
- Having personal tuition for an hour every weeknight for a month
- Having all your clothes except school clothes given to charity shops

READ

1 Samuel 11:1-11

GAME: BUILD A COW

This game works like 'build a beetle'. You will need to have cut up some paper into a set of simple shapes for each group. Each group will need:

- A cows head
- A cows body
- Four cows legs
- A tail
- An udder

Each group will also need a die. The groups roll the dice as fast as they can. If they roll a 1 then they get the cows body. From there they can start to add the other things as they roll the correct numbers: 2 for a head, 3 for a leg, 4 for a tail, 5 for an udder and rolling a 6 means losing one of the body parts! The first group to finish building their cow without cheating wins. You will need to give out sheets or write up on a big sheet of paper what body part they get for whichever numbers they roll. After the game remind the group about the passage they just read. In it Saul takes two oxen and cuts them into pieces, sending pieces throughout Israel.

OPENING QUESTIONS

The passage has a lot of threats in it. Firstly there is the way the Ammonites are threatening a city. What tremendous fear the people must feel. Saul, burning with God's anger then threatens his own people if they don't help the beseiged city!

- Think of a time when you've felt threatened by other people. How serious was it?
- Did Saul do the right thing by motivating the people through fear? What else could he have done?
- Do you think its ever right for us as Christians to threaten people?
- Should we ever be afraid of what might happen to us as Christians if we don't follow orders from our leaders or from God?

DRAMA: PROVE IT!

Split into small groups and give each group one of the following scenarios, or something similar. More than one group can use the same scenario. Give them a short while to come up with a drama based loosely on the theme (the more creative the drama and the ending the better!) and then get them to perform it back to the rest of the group.

One of you is determined to learn to play guitar but your family laugh at you and say that you always give things up easily. You're determined to prove them wrong!

One of you is trying to sell an amazing new product to the others but the others need some convincing that it really is worth their money.

One of you met a famous singer at a family party at the weekend and had a long conversation with them but your friends just won't believe you.

READ

1 Samuel 11:12-15

DISCUSSION: PROVING OURSELVES

The way Saul acts and the way the Ammonites are defeated gives the Israelites tremendous confidence in Saul's leadership. They ask to punish those who spoke doubt in the first place, but Saul isn't interested. He seems willing to forgive.

- Have we ever felt the need to try to prove ourselves at something?
- Can we remember a time when we succeeded? How about failing?
- How does it feel when people think we're not capable of something? What different ways can we respond? Maybe brainstorm these.
- How does it feel when we do succeed at something that our friends or family have doubted we could accomplish?

READ

1 Samuel 12:1-5 and 16-20

WORSHIP: CLEAN HANDS

Samuel states his innocence before the people of Israel and asks for anyone to bring charges if he has been dishonest or sinful in any way. Amazingly no-one does. Would we pass that test? What about if we asked here at cell? Then Samuel goes on to remind the Israelites that they sinned greatly when they rejected God's direct leadership by asking for a king. Sometimes we need to be reminded when we've sinned and have the opportunity to repent. Have a time of worship during which people are invited to wash their hands in a bowl in the centre of the room and ask for God's forgiveness for something they've done wrong. This could be done with quiet music in the background or as part of a time of sung worship. Depending how confident the group are, and how well they know each other you may ask them to pray their confessions out loud.

SESSION 8:
IMPATIENCE AND BRAVERY

SET THE SCENE

Remind the group how we saw Saul establish himself as a strong leader. He now is feeling confident in his role and may even be getting a little arrogant. Samuel meanwhile has taken a back seat and does very little. Today's story starts with a difficult decision for Saul.

ACTIVITY: IMPATIENT PUZZLES

Use a number of small puzzles (ball and maze puzzles, rubiks cube, etc) for this activity. Split the group into pairs or threes and give each of them one of the puzzles. See which group can get the puzzle finished quickest. They may claim the other groups puzzle was easier so feel free to swap the puzzles round at certain points to test that out. Explain that to solve the puzzles takes patience and today we are looking at one of Saul's flaws: impatience.

READ

1 Samuel 13:1-15

OPENING QUESTIONS

Saul does something rash because he is worried about the fact that people are afraid and are starting to leave.

- What do you think Saul was thinking?
- Was this necessarily wrong? Why or why not?
- What do you think you'd have done in his position?
- Have you ever done something rash out of impatience? Would you consider yourself a patient or impatient person?

WORSHIP: GOD'S TIMETABLE

Play some music quietly in the background and hand out a blank timetable that covers a week from Monday to Sunday, 6am to midnight. Ask the group to start colouring in or blocking out time that they spent on things last week: so school is likely to take most of the daytime Monday to Friday for instance. They should do this as quietly as possible. After they have had a while and as they continue to write, draw and colour their timetables start introducing the following ideas:

- Ask them to look at their week and think through where God was at work, or where they felt God's presence most in that week. What do they think God was doing? This is reflective – you're not asking for responses but you might consider getting them to mark their timetables with a star if there were times when God was really noticeably there. After a short quiet time for them to think about that you lead the group in a prayer of thanks for God's presence.
- Ask them to look at their week and think through the times that were really difficult, boring or stressful. They might want to mark these with an 'X' while you pray for God's help and support in these things.
- Ask them to look at what they really enjoyed: who they enjoyed being with, the things they did which were fun. Again, pray some thanks for friends and family.
- Ask them where they served or helped others. When did they put others needs before their own? Where did they do something to help parents or the church? Pray a suitable prayer about this.
- Ask them to identify what time they set aside for God last week. What time did they give to God? Pray that as a group we won't be impatient in our own worship but that we will make time for God and to wait on God.

After this, give time for the group to share their thoughts and feelings on how their timetables looked. Is there anything they need more prayer for, or anything they need to change? Are we as a group rushing our worship?

ACTIVITY: BRAVERY CHALLENGE

Use some disgusting foods and see who is brave enough to eat them. Ensure that they look and taste gross but check for allergies before doing this. You could also have a range of other challenges such as drinking coke that has been drained through a dirty sock or putting a worm down your boxers. See if you can discover who the bravest (or most stupid!) person in the group is.

READ

1 Samuel 14:1-14

DISCUSSION

This is an incredible story of bravery given that the rest of the Israelites are cowering in fear. Jonathan is Saul's son and it seems his heart is in the right place. Not only does he have incredible leadership qualities (v7) but he is willing to put his own life on the line. This may have something to do with the fact that his confidence is not in himself but in God (vs 10-12).

- Can you imagine how brave you would need to be to climb towards people who were saying 'come here and we'll teach you a lesson'? Have you ever had someone seriously threaten to physically beat you? How did you respond?
- Is there a difference between bravery and stupidity? How would we know which is which?
- Should we expect God to intervene if we do stupid things in his name?
- How would you define bravery? How brave would you say you were?

READ

1 Samuel 14:15-23

RESPONSE / CHALLENGE

Notice how this one small act of bravery changes the entire battle. God himself sends panic among the Philistines and brings victory for the Israelites. Sometimes it can appear as if a problem is too big for us to be able to solve but a small action in the right direction makes a massive difference. If someone is having problems at home (parents falling out, brother is hassling them, etc) or at school (not getting on with a teacher, friends arguing with each other, etc) or even at church then maybe there are a few small brave acts that we can do that might change the whole situation. We might not see how it will make a significant difference but with God one small action done with the right attitude makes a world of difference. Depending on the mood of the group a few people may want to share something they think they could do, or they might want to write it down, or you may just leave it for them to think about.

SESSION 9: ARROGANCE AND EXCUSES

SET THE SCENE

Remember what we have seen of Saul so far. After a good start we saw him begin to display signs of impatience and arrogance when he wouldn't wait for Samuel before carrying out a sacrifice. Today we see a crucial moment in Saul's life: the day he made a critical mistake that made God regret making him king.

GAME: SIMON SAYS

Play a quick game of simon says with the group. You may want the leader to have a water sprayer so anyone who is out gets sprayed. Some people are really good at this game so you may find you have several winners. At the end of the game explain that some people are better than others at following instructions.

READ

1 Samuel 15:1-11

OPENING QUESTIONS

It seems that Saul doesn't follow Samuel's instructions. This isn't about mercy, he still kills all the people. He keeps the good valuable stuff though. These verses contain some difficult instructions where God encourages whole families (including infants) to be killed. That might need a little unpacking.

- Why might God tell Saul to do this? Why would God want all the Amalekite people wiped out?
- Is it fair that people should be punished for something that previous generations did? Should you ever be judged on stuff your family or country have done generations before?
- More directly, why do you think Saul doesn't do as he's told?

ACTIVITY: CLAY MODELLING

Using either playdough or modelling clay get each member of the group to see if they can make a model of themselves. They could either make just thier head and face or they could try and do a full body sculpture! This is very difficult, especially with a small amount of clay but could be good fun. While people are finishing off their models ask the group what they would think if they walked into a friends room and found that they had sculpted a lifesize model of themselves! How strange would it be to put a statue of yourself up for everyone to see!

READ

1 Samuel 15:12-23

GAME: EXCUSES

All sit in a circle. Each player has to come up with an excuse for why they didn't do their homework. The excuses can be as ridiculous as they like but can't be the same or too similar to anyone elses. Move clockwise around the circle. If anyone can't think of an excuse or takes too long then they are out of the game and the others continue to play until there is only one winner. If you have time to play this more than once then you could also put different scenarios: why didn't you tidy your room, why is the dog missing, etc. Just have fun with it.

DISCUSSION

Saul has become unbelievably proud and arrogant. It seems that not only has he set up a statue of himself but he also now thinks he knows better than God! He makes excuse after excuse as to why he hasn't followed instructions. He seems to be a little dishonest in places, claiming he did do as he was told. Samuel has to remind him that God values certain things more than others, and obedience and humility are crucial for people to stay close to God. It's no good thinking that you can use worship as an excuse not to do what God says! Nothing could be worse! But we often encounter arrogance ourselves:

- Do we have any friends or teachers who we think are particularly arrogant? What makes us think of them that way?

- How arrogant would we think we are? On a scale of one to ten how much do you tend to assume you are better or more intelligent or more gifted than others?
- What are the real signs of arrogance? How can we spot if we are becoming too arrogant ourselves?

RESPONSE

Make sure you leave good time for this because it should be a really good and affirming thing for everyone in the group and to help to bond the group as a whole. One way we can prevent ourselves from becoming arrogant is to ensure that we recognise the amazing gifts and attitudes in the people around us. Tell the group that we are going to put some music on and split into pairs. Each person will tell the person they are paired with 'You're better than me at...' and will finish the sentence. Once they've done this (and it shouldn't take long) re-arrange the pairs. If you have time do it until everyone in the group has been in a pair with everyone else.

READ

1 Samuel 15:24-35

PRAYER / WORSHIP: THE PRODIGALS

Light a candle in the centre and place some unlit tea-lights near it. We see in this story the fact that Samuel is grieved that Saul has turned away from God. We may have friends who we are praying need to know Jesus. Now is a good time for us to pray for them and to ask God to begin to bring them into contact with the church. Encourage people to come forward, light a tea-light and say the name (with possibly a short prayer) for someone who they are worried about or hoping will soon come to faith.

SESSION 10: THE NEW KID

SET THE SCENE

Last week we saw how God rejected Saul as king because of his disobedience and arrogance. Saul was still technically king but God's attention turned elsewhere. Today we move to one of the better known stories of the Bible, that of the boy David who would himself later become king.

ACTIVITY: MAKE-OVER

Split the group into two teams and equip them with hair gel and possibly make up, etc. Each group find a volunteer and they have to try and make them look as good as possible! This isn't about vandalising their face, its very much about trying to make a radical difference to their appearance that makes them look really trendy. You may want to bring the models into the room one by one when they are finished and compare them. You will need to judge which group did the best job. The volunteers may want to clean themselves up!

READ

1 Samuel 16:1-13

OPENING QUESTIONS

Its really key to note the words in verse 7: people look at the outward appearance but God looks at the heart. David is so unlikely to be the one who is chosen to be king that he's not even present with the rest of the family. They have to fetch him from the fields. In a world which prizes image above everything we think that we can judge people by their appearance but the Bible tells us differently:

- How much time and attention do you give to your own appearance?
- Who do you know who spends hours on the way they look? Do you think that's a good thing or not?

- If appearance really doesn't matter at all then why are we told in verse 12 that David himself was handsome? What does this tell us? Is it important?
- Do we ever feel overlooked by others because they just don't think we're capable of doing certain things?
- Are we more welcoming as a group to good looking people? Do we find it harder to be friends with 'ugly' people?

ACTIVITY: TRUE / FALSE

We are now going to look at the story of David and Goliath. As the story is really well known play a game of true or false with the group to see how well they actually really do know it. Get them to stand up if they think something is true and to sit down if they think its false. Possible statements could include:

1. Goliath was over nine feet tall (True)
2. Goliath challenges the Israelites every day for seven days before David goes out to fight him (False – it was forty)
3. David is visiting his brothers with cheese when he sees what is happening (True)
4. King Saul has offered his daughter in marriage to whoever slays Goliath and will let them and their family off paying taxes. (True)
5. David goes to see the king and claims that he has killed both lions and bears while defending his father's sheep (True)
6. Saul initially laughs at David and won't let David fight Goliath, but the prophet Samuel tells him to so he gives in (False – Samuel's not even there!)
7. Saul tries to make David wear his armour but it just won't fit (True)
8. David takes a staff to fight Goliath with (True – as well as his sling!)
9. David takes seven stones from the stream to use in his sling (False – it was five)
10. David knocks Goliath out with a stone and then kills him with his own sword (False – the Bible says the stone killed him. The beheading was just for effect!)

GAME: TUG OF WAR

Either use some rope for this or just draw a line on the floor and get two members of the group to stand either side of the line and hold on to one of each others wrists. Then get them to tug each other and see who can get their partner over the line first. Ideally play this a few times and make sure some of the pairings are really unfair: match your biggest and strongest member against the smallest one. Explain that just like its obvious who is going to win it was obvious to everyone watching who would win the battle of David vs Goliath. But maybe there is still room for us to be shocked and surprised at the outcome!

READ

1 Samuel 17:1-31

DISCUSSION

David's only visiting when he sees Goliath challenging his brothers and the rest of the Israelite army. He's still too young to be there.

- Why do you think that his older brother gets so angry with him?
- Last session we looked at arrogance. Is David acting a bit arrogant? Why or why not?
- Do we ever get a real sense of confidence that we can do something but find it hard to convince others to give us the opportunities?
- Is there anything we'd like to do at church that we can't do because people see us as too young or too inexperienced?

GAME: ELASTIC SLINGSHOT

Split the group into smaller groups of around three people. Give each group a number of elastic bands and place three containers (pint glasses, flower pots or something similar but they must all be identical) at the other end of a room, or in another room through an open door. At the same time get the groups to start firing their elastic bands into their containers. See which group gets the most in and give them a prize. You may want to play this a few times, its quite addictive.

READ

1 Samuel 17:32-51

WORSHIP: FACING GIANTS

Spend some time in sung worship but make space for people to think about what areas of life God might want them to have real success in. What giants need to fall in our own lives? Discouragement, unfaith, jealousy, anger, unfaithfulness, addictions, etc? Do we have faith that God can do it? Will we step out in faith?

SESSION 11: THE GREEN-EYED MONSTER

SET THE SCENE

Remind the group where we are in the story of Saul and David. David has arrived on the scene and killed Goliath and Saul is delighted! The problem is solved. Today we see what happens between Saul and David after that.

ACTIVITY: GREEN-EYED MONSTER

Give everyone in the group a piece of paper and a black pen. Have a couple of green pens in the room as well that people can share between them. Tell everyone to draw a green-eyed monster but to keep their creations secret. After they have done this fold them all up, mix them up and hand them back out. No-one is to say if they have their own or someone elses. Then go round the group and get the group to try and guess who drew which ones. Explain that there is a particular emotion or feeling that is sometimes called 'the green-eyed monster'. It's jealousy and today we will be looking at how jealousy came into play between Saul and David.

READ

1 Samuel 18:1-16

OPENING QUESTIONS

Its amazing how quickly a good friendship turns sour when people start to get jealous but you can sort of see where Saul is coming from. His own son seems to love David, the crowds love David and they all think David is better than Saul.

- Was Saul still wrong to feel jealous of David?
- Is jealousy always wrong or is it sometimes ok? (after the group have answered this question you may like to point out that the NIV translation of Exodus 20:5 says 'I, the Lord your God, am a jealous God...', so is jealousy sometimes ok?)

- Have we ever felt jealous of someone else – could we share some of these stories now?
- Have we ever felt that other people were jealous of us and how did we respond? How should we respond?

READ

1 Samuel 18:17-30

GAME: WHAT'S IT WORTH?

Bring in a number of items that you've bought from a supermarket. Split the group into pairs or threes. Bring out the items one by one and get each group to guess a price (you might want to get them to write it down before reading it out so that they don't copy each others). Then let them know the actual price of the item and allocate points to the groups accordingly. Move on to the next item. The group with the most points at the end wins. Explain that some things are clearly worth more than others but what is the perfect boyfriend or girlfriend worth? Saul tries to get David killed by setting an impossible price on his daughter but David is willing to even pay double that!

READ

1 Samuel 19:1-17

GAME: BED DECEPTION

Split the group into at least two smaller groups, possibly more. This game involves a duvet (the bigger the better). One group goes first. Either one of the group members hides under the duvet or pillows are arranged under it to look like there is a group member hiding there. The other group are then brought into the room while any remaining members of the first group go elsewhere. They have to decide if it is a person or a fake person. Play this at least three times and then swap the groups around. The team who got most of the guesses correct wins. You could make this more interesting by insisting that one small part of the body / dummy must be visible outside the duvet (the end of a shoe, some hair, etc), or by trying to get the groups to guess which person is under there. Explain that its not always easy to tell when we are being deceived in this situation. Saul's own daughter Michal plays this game to protect her husband David from her father.

DISCUSSION

Saul seems to be losing his grip on his own feelings and actions. The people who know and love him give him good advice and persuade him to leave David alone which he does for a while but then very suddenly he turns on David and attacks him. The truth is that Saul is not accountable to anyone and has lost control.

- Are there any people whose advice we listen to?
- What about when they tell us to do stuff we don't want to do?
- Why does Saul try to kill David after saying he won't do that?
- Do we ever make a decision to do something and then do the exact opposite?
- How do we know if we have our own feelings under control?
- When was the last time we did something because we felt like doing it even though we knew in our heads we'd regret it?

Explain that as Christians we should all be accountable to someone. That means there are a couple of people who we implicitly trust and whose advice we respect. We hopefully even respect them enough to do what they advise sometimes in the face of our own feelings or desires.

READ

1 Samuel 19:18-24

WORSHIP: PROPHECY

Note in the passage how even people who turn up with hostile intentions to arrest David get overwhelmed by a spirit of prophecy when they get close to the prophets. Explain that prophecy isn't just for people who are 'prophets'. All Christians can engage in prophecy at times, and we need to practice it or make space for it to happen. Place some objects in the middle of the room (such as some different pieces of fruit, a flower, a leaf, a book, a musical instrument, some perfume, some food, jewellery, an ipod, anything in fact – the more the better!). Play some quiet background music and talk the group through how we can encourage one another through prophecy. Then pick an item and speak to someone in the group using it (eg. the perfume may speak about someone's prayers being like sweet-smelling perfume to God, or it might speak about someone's humble character being attractive like perfume). Encourage the other members of the group to do the same, encouraging each other with words in this way. Explain that you can use the same object more than once.

SESSION 12: GUY LOVE?

SET THE SCENE

After a good start things between David and Saul have turned sour. That's because Saul is jealous of David and seems to want to kill him. Saul however is going a little crazy at this point. He seems to sometimes be nice to David and sometimes to passionately hate him. Whatever Saul is up to he is clever enough to realise that even his own family seem to be siding with David and with every passing day his jealousy is only getting worse.

ACTIVITY: TREASURE HUNT

Split the group into two smaller groups and prepare a couple of small treasure hunts around the meeting place. Put some of the clues in code to make it a little more interesting. You could do this by simply using cryptic wording or you could assign each letter to a number (so A is 1, B is 2, etc) so they have to decode the clues properly. Get the groups to race against each other to complete their treasure hunt. Have a prize at the end for the winning team. Explain that just like we used coded or cryptic wording for the treasure hunt a special code is used in today's story between David and Jonathan.

READ

1 Samuel 20

OPENING QUESTIONS

David and Jonathan have a really close friendship. In terms of wordly ambition they should be enemies: Jonathan should be the next king and David is his main threat. But Jonathan has better values than that and he loves David.

- Do we think we'd sacrifice our own futures for those of our friends? How many friends do we have that we'd do this for?

- Have we ever had friends that our parents really dislike? How do we handle it when our parents and friends don't get on? What should we do?
- It seems that David and Jonathan might even be more than best friends. Some people think there might be something a little homosexual about the relationship they had. What do you think? If either of them were gay would that change anything?

GAME: BOWS AND ARROWS

Jonathan had to be pretty accurate to get his arrows in the right place so he could warn David about Saul's anger. If you can get hold of some plastic bows and arrows see if you can have a competition as to who can shoot them most on target. You may want to do this up a stairwell in a house, or across a garden.

READ

1 Samuel 21:1-9

DISCUSSION

David flees from Saul and runs to a priest for help. However he doesn't tell the priest that he's on the run. He instead tells a number of lies.

- Why is Ahimelech afraid when he meets David?
- Why do you think David lies to Ahimelech?
- When was the last time we told a lie? How often do we lie about small things? What about big things?
- Is it ever acceptable to lie or is it always sinful?

VIDEO CLIP

You may want to use video clip from either 'Liar, liar' or from 'The invention of lying', both of which show quite dramatically what can happen when we feel compelled to tell the truth at all times! Often people's feelings get hurt! So what should a Christian attitude to lying or telling the truth really be?

WORSHIP: HONESTY

Often we say things in worship which we don't really mean, or don't really feel. That can be ok because we are just joining in with songs that the whole church are singing, or because we *want* to feel the things we say we are feeling. However in this section of worship make time for people to say or write very short prayers that are totally honest. Just tell God how you really feel or what you really need right now. Pray to him honestly not saying things that you think he might just want to hear or which might impress others.

READ

1 Samuel 21:10-15

DRAMA: INTERVIEW INSANITY

Note from the passage how David once again goes to great lengths to deceive the people he's with. Some people in a neighboring country recognise him so he tries to convince them there is no way he could actually be the famous David because he is just a crazed madman! It can't be easy to act insane like that! Split the group into smaller groups and give each one the following scenario to act out:

> You are at an interview that your parents have made you go to. You really don't want the job so have decided to act a bit crazy at the interview so you don't get it. The rest of your group should act as the interview panel. Make the scene as amusing as you can.

CHALLENGE

Ask the group to consider sharing something really honest this week with someone they trust. Ask them to try really hard to increase their level of honesty and integrity in what they say and do.

SESSION 13: ON THE RUN

ACTIVITY: ROAD SIGNS

Print off a selection of ten or fifteen road signs around the room, some of which might be well known and some of which are less well known. Each road sign should have a number. Split the group into pairs and give each pair a pen and some paper to write down what they think each sign means. When they have all done this get them to swap answer sheets and mark each others. Read out what the answers are and you may want to give a small prize to the winner. Explain that we will be using the road signs a little later as today we are thinking a bit about direction.

SET THE SCENE

David and Saul have now definitely parted ways. David is very much on the run having discovered that Saul is out to kill him. David has had to lie and deceive people in order to stay safe. He has had to leave all his friends and his home comforts and to become an outlaw. Meanwhile Saul is still the king and is using all his resources to find David and finish him off.

READ

1 Samuel 22:1-5

OPENING QUESTIONS

David begins to gather people around him and become something of an outlaw. Despite this he still seems keen to listen to God for direction, and seems willing to head wherever God leads.

- Are we the sort of people who are fairly decisive or do we take forever to make decisions about something?
- Do we tend to follow our common sense about stuff or are we more likely to have a gut feeling or a spiritual nudge?

- Have we ever asked for God's direction or answer about something? When was the last time we did this?
- Is there anything we'd like God's direction on now? Is there something we should be asking God about or would we prefer him to mind his own business?

WORSHIP: DIRECTION

Have a time of sung worship but also place the selection of road signs around the room. Ask the group to think about an area of life which they might like to have some direction about. Maybe its about a relationship or friendship, maybe about school options, university choices or the future. The road signs are there to help us to think about what God might be saying to us in life about those questions. Just take a look at each and think about what it might mean with regard to the question you are asking. See if any just feel right. You may want to give the group some time to share their thoughts at the end. Be aware that this activity is likely to work well for some members of the group but some (especially younger members) may just not get it at all.

READ

1 Samuel 22:6-23

DISCUSSION

Saul is trying desperately to regain control of the country and of his own men. He resorts partly to bribery and partly to fear. He offers all kinds of rewards for people who are loyal to him and Doeg is happy to accept. Meanwhile those who are seen to be siding with David are killed, even if they seem to have reasonable excuses and even if they are priests so most soldiers wouldn't dare to kill them!

- Has anyone ever tried to bribe us or to force us to tell them something they wanted to know? What happened?
- What kinds of ways do we try to gain power over other people? Do we ever try to use bribery or fear as tactics?
- Is it ever right or ok to try to manipulate other people or to persuade them to tell you things? How do you know if you are doing this in the right way or not?
- Who are we loyal to? Are there particular people who we think we would never betray?

Note how David at the end of the chapter takes responsibility for his own part in this. Unlike Saul who seems to think everything is everyone elses fault David seems to take more of the blame than he really deserves.

- When we do things wrong are we willing to take the blame for them?
- In complicated situations do we tend to pass the buck or do we own up for the part we played in it all?

GAME: ASKING DIRECTION

This game is played by blindfolding someone and having someone else guide them around a number of objects (eg. chairs, etc). The blindfolded person has to ask questions of their partner in order to work their way forward. Their partner (who can see) can only answer 'yes' or 'no'. So the blindfolded person may say 'should i take a step forward' and the only answer can be 'yes' or 'no'. If the blindfolded person hits any object you could spray them with a water sprayer. Also, if the speaker says something they are not allowed to then you could spray them. You could also have two sets of pairs doing this as a race to make it more interesting. Explain that one of the key differences between Saul and David is the way in which David repeatedly seeks God's direction in every decision. He asks of God whether he should go or stay and where he should go. He seems hesitant to do anything unless he knows what God wants. What an incredible example for us. Check this out in the following reading.

READ

1 Samuel 23:1-14

GAME: MANHUNT

Depending on where you are meeting, the weather conditions and the time you have available you may want to consider playing a quick game of manhunt in a garden. One or more of the group go and hide and the rest have to find them in the quickest time possible. There are different versions of this game which is basically a variation of 'hide and seek', some of which involve those caught then helping the others to find whoever is left. Summarise at the end of the game by saying that David is basically on the run and in hiding from Saul for some time. The difference is that if he gets caught then he will die. Imagine what that must feel like!

SESSION 14: DIFFICULT DECISIONS

SET THE SCENE

Saul is now hot in pursuit of David but David keeps evading him. David is being forced to camp out like an outlaw with a motley group of disaffected Israelites. However his heart is still in the right place and we saw last session how David still seeks God's direction and guidance in all the decisions he makes.

GAME: STEALTH

Ideally this game is played in a fairly large room though it can work ok in a smaller one. One person stands in the middle of the room and is blindfolded. They have a small piece of cloth (such as a duster) tucked in to the top of their trousers at the back. Another person is picked to sneak up on them and try to steal the duster. The blindfolded person can't hold on to the duster or make it impossible to steal but they can move as much as they like. If they manage to tag the person who is sneaking up on them then that person is out and has to return to their seat. Another person is then chosen. This game is just for fun so don't worry if it is hard to referee or if people develop strategies to ensure they win! Explain that in the passages we're looking at during this session David uses stealth to sneak up on Saul and we see what happens when he does.

READ

1 Samuel 24

OPENING QUESTIONS

David has every opportunity to kill Saul but refuses to do so, even though his men are urging him on.

- Why doesn't David take this opportunity to kill Saul?
- Why does David feel guilty about having cut off some of Saul's cloak?

- Do we ever disrespect people who God has put in authority over us? What should our response to this be?
- Do you think David did the right thing?
- Are we ever pressured by our friends to do things we might regret? What kind of things are we under pressure about at the moment?

READ

1 Samuel 25:1-22

DEBATE: THE PROTECTION RACKET

The story in this chapter is a little difficult to unpack! David basically protects Nabal's men for a while but then demands some charity from Nabal as a result. Nabal says that its not a deal he's made or is interested in. Who is in the right here? Have a debate by splitting the group into half. Each half are given one of the following viewpoints to defend. Allow the group to get heated about this if they want – there are some dubious ethics at work here!

You are to defend Nabal. David's men are offering something like a mafia protection racket. Nabal is just minding his own business and David demands that he gives him free food and supplies for no reason whatsoever! No wonder Nabal says no. As a result David resorts to physical violence, intending to kill Nabal and his men just because they didn't give him some free stuff. How can that be right or fair? Nabal never asked for David's protection!

You are to defend David. David has done everything he can to help out a neighbour, defending their possessions and ensuring that they are kept safe. He is polite and respectful and offers only peace and friendship. In return Nabal just insults David's men. Nabal is clearly a mean-spirited, greedy, selfish individual who needs to be taught a lesson. Besides, anyone who turns away someone who is so clearly in need should be punished in some way!

READ

1 Samuel 25:23-44

DISCUSSION

Clearly Abigail saves the situation! Note that the ethics are still very debatable. While God seems initially to side with David by killing off Nabal – probably more because of his general attitude than his specific action of refusing to offer support – David also acknowledges now that for him to have killed Nabal would also have been wrong (v.39).

- Is it always wrong to fail to offer support to those who are in need?
- How do we react to homeless people on the streets?
- How do we respond when friends at school ask us if they can have or borrow stuff that's ours because they really need it? When did this last happen?
- Are we ever really proud or rude to others? How do we tend to respond to new people or strangers – are we aloof or unwelcoming?
- What can we do to ensure we have the right attitude to other people?

WORSHIP: PHONE SACRIFICE

Have a time of worship during which the group members will need their mobile phones. Light a candle in the centre and during some quiet time ask them to think about the text messages that they have sent and received during the week and the other things that might be stored on the phone. They may even want to scroll through their 'sent messages' to think about this. What do the messages we've sent say about us? What might God think about the way we deal with others? Are we rude or proud or acting in a sinful way? Ask people to place their phones in the centre if they would like to ask God to help them act with more integrity in the way they use their phones. Pray that God will help us to use our phones to bless and encourage others rather than anything else.

GAME: SLEEPING LIONS

This is a well-known game that is still good fun with older teens. Everyone pretends to be totally asleep (or dead!) except for one person whose job it is to look for any movement at all. They can try to make the others laugh or move in some way, gradually doing things that make it harder and harder for the others to stay still (eg. poking them, etc). See who in the group is able to stay 'asleep' in such difficult circumstances.

READ

1 Samuel 26

CHALLENGE

We often seek revenge on people who do wrong to us and today we saw how David refuses to take revenge on Saul but almost makes an error by seeking revenge on Nabal. Holding grudges is a difficult and destructive thing. Jesus tells us as Christians we have to forgive those who wrong us and not hold grudges. Encourage the group to think carefully about a person who they really don't get on with or who they hold a grudge with. Challenge them to make an effort this week to put things right – to say sorry or to seek to build bridges with that person.

SESSION 15: THE DARK SIDE

SET THE SCENE

David's now been running from Saul for a long time. He's tired and worn out. He needs somewhere to settle for a while. Saul meanwhile continues to go from bad to worse. It seems to simply be too late for him to change the way things are going to turn out.

GAME: TWISTER

Play a few games of twister as a group, or allow a few people to play at a time. See who is best at manoevring their opponents off the board! Explain that today we will be looking both at political manoevring and also at our need for space to settle and space of our own. We'll also be looking at how some spiritual stuff can be somewhat 'twisted' and thinking through our response to that.

READ

1 Samuel 27

OPENING QUESTIONS

We see in this passage how David goes for a while to live with some of Israel's enemies: the Philistines! These were the people who had fought the Israelites when David was a boy in the whole David vs Goliath incident. Somehow David finds favour in the eyes of their leader and convinces him to let his people settle in the town of Ziklag.

- Do you think David must have found it difficult to befriend the Philisitines? Why would he do this?
- Have you ever had to change your views about someone you hated? Have you ever had to ask a favour from someone you disliked?
- Do you think David is compromising his integrity?

- Why does David hide the truth from Achish about his raids on the surrounding lands? Is it ok for him to be lying in this way?
- Do you ever desperately need your own space? What lengths do you go to for some time or space of your own?

QUIZ: LEADERS IN DISGUISE

Print off some pictures of famous world leaders, sports personalities, film stars and the like and disguise their faces by drawing on hats, scarves, beards, glasses, etc. Hand them out to the group and see if they can correctly identify the leaders. Explain that Saul finds a reason to disguise himself in today's passage.

READ

1 Samuel 28:3-8

ACTIVITY: GHOST STORY

Ask the group why Saul disguises himself. Also ask if they think that the consulting a medium is likely to bring about any success? Explain that for the rest of today's session we are going to be looking at the question of whether Christians believe in things like ghosts. This activity may take quite a bit of time and can be done in several ways. You could split the group into smaller groups and simply ask each group to come up with and act out some sort of ghost story. If the group aren't all that dramatic they may prefer just to come up with a ghost story to be read out rather than acted. Or if you have the equipment you may even want to try to make a short ghost story video clip. If they are short on ideas and you are able to prepare far enough in advance you may want to show them a short piece of a TV programme of the 'Most Haunted' variety where people seek out ghosts in old buildings. After you have spent some time having fun with a ghost related theme then explain that today's passage contains an appearance of a ghost in the Bible!

READ

1 Samuel 28:8-25

DISCUSSION

This is a very unexpected part of the Old Testament! Saul in desperation for some guidance reaches a new moral low and turns to the dark spiritual side by consulting with a medium. Mediums are people who claim to be able to speak to the souls of those who are already dead. Amazingly we are told that the woman he speaks to does indeed summon the spirit of the now-dead prophet Samuel who tells Saul that he is doomed.

- Do we believe in ghosts? Should Christians believe in ghosts?
- Are you aware of anyone who has started playing with the occult (ouija boards, tarot cards, horoscopes, spells, etc). Have we ever been tempted or drawn in to doing these things?
- Do we tend to think of the devil as being at work as well as God? Have we ever been afraid of something we've seen or encountered?

Give this discussion plenty of time. The group may want to explore some of these issues in depth. Ensure that you deal sensitively with their experiences. Explain that Christians think that dealing with the occult is dangerous, and its dangerous because its real. Some people may just be conmen but others really are dealing with dangerous spiritual power. However Jesus will protect us and set us free from any hold the devil has on us if we simply ask him to.

RESPONSE / WORSHIP

Sing some songs that emphasise God's power over those of the world or the devil. During the time of worship offer to pray prayers of freedom and protection over each cell member. Something very short and positive works well. For instance you may want to pray 'Father, protect *name* from the enemy and fill them with your Spirit.' If you have picked up that a member of the group has had a lot of experience of the occult you may want to talk and pray with them about this separately as well after the meeting or on another occasion.

SESSION 16: STABBED IN THE BACK

SET THE SCENE

We saw last session how David and his band of several hundred followers have settled with the Philistines who are still Israel's enemies. In fact the Israelites and the Philistines are about to have a major battle which is why Saul wanted to consult a medium. Saul now seems to be resigned to his fate. This week we see the end of this legend and see David continuing to act in a confusing manner. This week we come to the end of the book of first Samuel.

READ

1 Samuel 29

OPENING QUESTIONS

David seems to be keen to go into battle on the side of the Philistines but it seems strange that he would do this having made such a point of not harming Saul in the past!

- Do you think that David intended to betray Achish?
- Would it have been ok for David to betray Achish?
- Have we ever felt betrayed by someone? Have we ever felt the need to betray someone even in a minor way?
- Do you think God would ever ask us to let out another person's secret or to in some way betray their confidence? Would God ever ask us to betray friends or family or the people we work for? And would we do it?

Regardless of what David's intentions were the other Philistines don't trust him and his men anyway so insist that Achish sends them back. Achish reluctantly does so. David may have been disappointed at this point, thinking that his very cunning plan might have failed (if he did intend to turn on Achish in the battle).

ACTIVITY: THE TRAY GAME

Prepare a tray with at least twenty-five objects on it, ideally more. The objects can be anything (cutlery, ornaments, stationery – anything small!). Leave the tray in a different room to where the group meet until you are ready to use it then bring it through. Leave it in the room for one minute and tell the group to memorise everything that is on the tray. Then remove the tray from the room. Hand out paper and pens and ask the group members to write down everything they can remember that was on the tray. See who can remember the most things. Then bring the tray back in and see what they forgot! Explain that when David and his men return home from the Philistine battle party they discover that a few things have gone missing...

READ

1 Samuel 30

DISCUSSION

How quickly things change! From thinking that his own plan has been spoiled David discovers that his own hometown of Ziklag has been attacked. If Achish hadn't sent them back then they would never have got there in time to rescue their families and get their possessions back.

- David is not popular with his men when they find out what happened. They seem to turn on him. When in life have we felt particularly friendless or unpopular? How did we handle this?
- We are told that David found strength in God. How do you think he did this? Do we ever do this and if so how?
- David once again seeks direction from God even in his distress. Do you think its easier to seek God's direction when things are going well or when they go badly? Why?
- The men are so exhausted not all of them have the energy to fight. Those who do fight want to keep the plunder from those who don't but David insists they share. Is this fair?

WORSHIP: STRENGTH FROM GOD

Split the group into threes and ask them to find some space to listen to each other's needs and to pray for each other. They may want to particularly think about how they are getting on with friends at the moment or what areas of life they particularly would value God's help with. Try to ensure that the each group has at least one person in it who will be able to lead the others in praying if they lack some confidence or focus.

GAME: BALLOON WAR

For this game you will need to get the group to inflate and tie the ends of a number of balloons. Then split the group into two smaller groups. Each group is assigned balloons of a certain colour (so one group may have blue and red balloons and the other group may have green and yellow balloons for instance). All balloons start on the floor in the middle of the room. When you say 'go' each group must try to burst the other group's balloons and protect their own balloons. Whichever group bursts all the other group's balloons first wins. This is obviously a very loud game and needs to be played in a room with a minimum number of things that can be broken! After the game explain that we all know that real battles are not fun. The final chapter of first Samuel ends in misery for Saul and the Israelites.

READ

1 Samuel 31

DEBATE: EUTHANASIA

Depending on the time you have left and the people in your group you may want to have a debate about whether it is ever acceptable for people to kill themselves or other people. Saul knows that he's doomed and asks his armor-bearer to kill him. In the end he has to fall on his sword himself because the armor-bearer is too scared to do the deed. You can encourage a debate by splitting the group into two and having one group arguing for mercy killing and the other half arguing against, or you could just let people put forward their own opinions which may be more worthwhile with a complicated subject like this! Try to be sensitive to those who may have experience with this area and try to avoid being judgmental regardless of what your personal theological views are.

FINISHING THE SERIES

Following all sixteen of these sessions you may like to have a session to summarise the whole book in some way. The best way to do this could be to have a quiz together to see who can remember the most from the story. You may also want to have time to reflect on what each member of the group has learned most from the series as a whole.

Sometimes in our youth work setting we have actually sat the young people down to do an exam on the subject! Strange as this may sound many of them enjoy this as it takes seriously the subject matter and shows them in a playful way that what they are learning is meaningful and worth remembering.

So much depends on the young people concerned. But be sure that you don't just let the sessions drift off. There should be some sort of definite end or celebration. Working all the way through a book of the Bible is an achievement especially when it is one of the longer ones such as 1 Samuel!

You will also be wanting to think about what the group may want or need to study next. Don't allow the group to lose momentum now that they are engaging so creatively with the Bible.

ABOUT THE AUTHOR

Paul Franklin is the Youth Minister for the Whitstable Team Ministry, a group of six Anglican churches in Kent. He spends most of his time pastoring and leading the youth congregation 'Y' and helping co-ordinate other youth groups in the parish. He has been in his current post for over eight years mainly because no-one else is likely to employ him since the jelly and barbed wire incident (and while it is true that Paul was somewhat to blame for the injuries the young person received it is also true that this particular young person will never forget just how dangerous real Bible study can be).

Paul is always working on new projects and has recently published a short course to introduce young people to Christianity called 'cool beans'. He has also worked with some of the young people at 'Y' to publish a very amusing panto script called 'Into the Stationery Cupboard' which can help larger youth groups build community and engage in mission. Both of these are available on www.amazon.com.

Paul lives and works with the 'New Ground' gap year team which supports students and gap year volunteers while they use their gifts to bless the churches and young people in Whistable while they get experience in youth work and ministry. The volunteers receive free accommodation and some money for food and support. They are always looking for new volunteers for the team and details can be found at www.whitstable-live.org. Some volunteers are full-time students at universities based in Canterbury and living and working with the team really helps to make their studies more affordable.

In his spare time Paul likes to play sports badly, to try to learn how to buy i-tunes and to watch endless episodes of Property Ladder, Midsomer Murders and Battlestar Galactica. Please pray for him.

www.ingramcontent.com/pod-product-compliance
Ingram Content Group UK Ltd.
Pitfield, Milton Keynes, MK11 3LW, UK
UKHW041915190726
13854UKWH00003B/1255